Also by Judy Barnes

Born to Be King of the World

His Unconditional Love

Two Girls from Nazareth

MARY MAGDALEN

JUDY BARNES

ISBN
978-1-959365-02-0 (Paperback)
978-1-959365-03-7 (eBook)

Table of Contents

Preface

I decided to try to write a book about Mary Magdalen. Easy, right? I knew there wasn't a lot written about her in the King James Version of the New Testament. So I decided to look on the internet. I found a lot of information. Strangely enough, almost all of it was written several centuries after she had died.

She was described by some writers as an apostle, as Jesus's closest and most beloved disciple and the only one who truly understood his teachings.

I expected to use a lot of my imagination. I always do, but it turns out, I had to use more of my imagination along with a lot of Heavenly guidance, in order to accomplish my task.

Mary was born in Magdala. For some reason she was called Mary Magdalen. Nobody knows what her last name really was. Was everyone from Magdala given the last name of Magdalen? Strange. Maybe it was because there were so many Mary's in the New Testament. Maybe it was a way to distinguish between them. However, the only other Mary sister of Martha of any consequence was Mary the mother of Jesus. Was that the reason? I guess we will never know.

Judy Barnes

Chapter One
MAGDALA

M agdala was a city on the west side of the Sea of Galilee. The small city was known for preserving fish. Sometimes they used salt to preserve the fish. Other times they were pickled. The pickled fish of Galilee were known throughout the Roman and Greek world. Large quantities were taken up to Jerusalem at the season of the yearly feasts, because of the great multitudes of people. Barrels were also transported around the Mediterranean. Because it was a port on the Sea of Galilee, it was a center of trade and commerce, and an exporter of salted fish to markets as far away as Europe.

Magdala was also a place for shipbuilding. There were many people who were artists at building ships.

People of that era were very wealthy because they were hard workers and had commodities that were in high demand.

Magdala had some baths with hot water from an underground hot spring. Those baths were used for purification. It was called living water rather than rainwater.

Magdala had a very ornate Synagogue. It was decorated with brightly colored frescoes. It was evident that the people were wealthy.

The women had for their use perfume jars, jewelry, hairbrushes and combs and bronze applicators of make-up.

* * * * *

"Thomas, I think my time has come. Please, go and get Barbara. She is a very competent mid-wife. She has been here for all of our babies births. Please hurry."

"Are you sure it is time?"

"Of course. This is baby number four. I am accustomed to knowing the signs", Margaret stated. She was getting a little bit aggravated. She knew what it felt like to go into labor.

"Boys, go over to grandmother's house. Plan on staying for a couple of days", their mother commanded. They were good boys. They would not be any trouble for Thomas' mother. Margaret loved her mother-in-law and knew the boys would be well taken care of.

It seemed like Thomas was gone a long time. Margaret's contractions were getting stronger. This baby is in a hurry.

Finally, Barbara walked into the house with all of the necessary items for the big event.

She had a big smile on her face, "Well, Margaret, are you going to have another boy?"

Margaret frowned, "Probably. That seems to be all I can make."

"But they are handsome boys and Thomas can teach them the fishing business, especially preservation. There is a high demand for that", Barbara said.

"Ooh, the pain is getting worse. He better be born soon. He seems to be taking his time", Margaret admitted.

"Here, put this damp cloth between your teeth and bear down when you have a really bad pain."

Barbara was a great mid-wife. She knew the right things to say when the pain was excruciating.

Margaret did not think she could trust anyone else with delivering her precious child.

Barbara asked, "What are you going to name this baby?"

"I hope it does not take much longer. This is getting bad," Margaret cried out.

The mid-wife motioned for Thomas to leave the room and shut the door. It was time. She helped the mother sit on the edge of the bed. She could see the head trying to make its way into the world. Barbara gently turned the baby's head to be in the right position.

"About two good pushes and your baby will have arrived", Barbara smiled.

It only took one good push and the mid-wife shrieked, "Oh, Margaret, you have a fine baby girl."

The mother could not believe her ears, "What did you say?"

"You have a fine baby girl", Barbara repeated herself.

"This cannot be true. A baby girl. Let me see her."

Barbara said, "Let me wash her and swaddle her first."

"No, I want to see her now."

"Thomas, come here", the new mother yelled to be heard in the next room.

The father entered the room. "What is wrong?"

"Nothing. We have a wonderful, beautiful baby girl", Margaret whispered.

"I do not believe it. After all these years…... a baby girl. She *is* beautiful," Thomas said softly. "The boys will be so surprised," Thomas announced.

He picked her up and proceeded to kiss her head and hands and her stomach.

Barbara stated, "She has not been washed, anointed and swaddled yet."

"I do not care. I just want to hold her for a few minutes," said the father.

Then he said excitedly, "I must go and tell her brothers."

Margaret smiled when her husband said that.

He handed the baby back to Barbara for the cleaning and the ritual to be performed as the baby is being prepared for her life.

Margaret had fallen asleep. Giving birth takes a lot of work. Every mother needs a nap after an ordeal like that.

Thomas crept out the door quietly as not to disturb mother or child.

* * * * *

As the father entered his mother's house he saw the boys sitting on the floor playing quietly with a puzzle.

Thomas junior looked up to see his father grinning. Is the baby born all ready? Have you seen him? Is he wonderful?

Thomas walked over to his mother and gave her a big kiss on the cheek. He then picked her up and twirled her around.

Then he announced, "We have a beautiful baby girl."

Johanna got so excited that she squealed, "That is wonderful…... a baby girl."

Amos ran to his father, "Really? Is that true?"

"It is true, Son. A baby girl."

Alexander just sat on the floor staring.

"Alexander, why are you not saying anything? You should be happy that we finally have a girl."

The boy looked up at his father with tears in his eyes, "A girl."

"Have you thought of a name for her? Amos asked.

"I do not think so. We figured it would be another boy", the father remarked.

The grandmother grinned. "You could name her Johanna. That's a fine strong name."

"You are right. Johanna is a great name. Being named for a great woman."

Johanna blushed.

Thomas said, "Margaret and I will have to talk about it. It will have to be a special name for a special little girl. I need to get back to the new mother."

The man opened the door and quickly retreated.

* * * * *

On the way back to the newest member of the family, Thomas told everyone he saw, the good news about the baby girl. The people congratulated him and shook his hand and hugged him tightly. They were all excited that Thomas and Margaret now were able to welcome a beautiful baby girl into the family.

All of the males in the family would dote on the little girl. There was no doubt about that. She would be carried around until she was able to walk.

They would play pat-a-cake and twirl her around until she was dizzy. Then they would laugh hard watching her trying to get her momentum.

* * * * *

As Thomas approached his home, he heard the baby crying.

He thought to himself (*That sounds like a good healthy cry*) and he smiled. He walked into the house and looked at his wife. "Why are you crying?"

Tears were streaming down her cheeks. "This baby has not quit crying since you left."

"Maybe she missed her father", and he laughed as he bent over to look at the child. "Is she wet or hungry?"

"No, I have taken care of all that. I do not know what is wrong, but she keeps on crying. I am tired and I need some sleep."

Thomas picked his daughter up and walked with her. He bounced her just a little bit thinking the movement might calm her down.

That did not work. She just cried all the time except when she was being fed or sleeping.

Unfortunately, she did not drink or sleep often enough. When she was sleeping, was the only time Margaret could sleep. She was not able to do any household chores. Either Thomas or other women in the area fixed the food, so that the father and the boys had food to eat. It seemed as though Thomas was losing weight. Margaret did not look very healthy.

The parents took the baby to the Synagogue when she was eight days old to be given a name and a blessing. Her name was Mary. She cried through the whole ritual.

The Rabbi told the parents that he thought she was harboring an Evil Spirit. He said he would give Mary a blessing to rid her of the Evil Spirit.

That did not work. He did not know what else to do, so he said he would pray for her and her family.

The family also prayed to have the Evil Spirit removed.

Thomas had heard of a woman in the city who was expert in removing Evil Spirits from people.

The father found Anna, and asked her to come to the house and send the Evil Spirit out of Mary and into Lake Galilee.

The boys were spending less time at home, because Mary's crying was very irritating. Thomas was working later when he could so he would be able to stay away from the house. Everyone was miserable.

Margaret would put Mary on a blanket on the floor so the baby could look around. Mary still cried.

Johanna would come and take Mary for a walk. When she brought her back they were both crying.

None of their friends came to see them. They did not want to listen to Mary crying.

Margaret tried taking her to the Synagogue on the Sabbath. Mary cried so much that her mother got embarrassed and took her home. The whole family was sorry that she had been taken, even though Margaret and Mary were in the Women's Gallery.

When she was getting close to a year old, she started crawling on her hands and knees. Finally, she quit crying. Because she was able to get around on her own, she was exploring her new world. She was so busy looking at everything, she did not cry anymore.

However, she found something else she could do to torment the family and any other person she could come in contact with.

She had quit crying, now she was biting. The family tried to keep her away from outsiders. She would bite for no apparent reason. And she bit HARD. She did not know she was doing anything wrong. The people in the family tried to tell her not to do it because she was hurting others.

One day, a few years later, a little girl named Madelyn came to the door.

Margaret answered. "Mary, Madelyn is here. She wondered if you would come out and play."

Mary got excited.

Madelyn was a nice little girl that lived just a couple of houses from Mary and her family.

Madelyn asked, "Would you like to go down by the wharf and watch the fishermen?"

"Yes, that sounds like fun," Mary responded.

The girls hurriedly walked near the Sea of Galilee.

The men were busy emptying the nets of fish. The fish had to be sorted so they could be put into separate barrels according to the kind and size.

The girls stayed back a little bit as to not get in the way. They watched excitedly. They had not been that close before.

The men were busy and were not paying attention to the girls.

Mary said, "We should go closer to watch. I do not think the men will mind."

"I do not think we should. The men might get mad," Madelyn said loudly.

One of the men said, "You girls get out of here. You might get hurt."

Mary retorted, "We will not get in the way. We just want to watch."

"Leave, we do not want you here. Go home and play."

Madelyn took Mary's hand and started pulling the girl away from the fishermen. Suddenly, Mary took Madelyn's hand and bit her hard. The girls hand started bleeding and she let out a shriek that would scare anyone.

Madelyn pulled away from Mary. Her hand was bleeding profusely. She ran home with Mary following behind.

When the girls neared their homes, they separated.

Madelyn's mother took one look at the blood and asked what had happened.

After the girl's mother heard the story, she marched her daughter to Mary's house.

Margaret answered the knock on the door. Mary hid around the corner.

Madelyn's mother exclaimed, "Look what your terrible child did to my daughter."

Margaret called to Mary, "Come here. Why did you do this to a little girl who wanted to play with you?"

Mary cried, "She pulled on my hand and I did not want to go with her."

"I want you to apologize to Madelyn."

"No, she was mean to me. She should not have pulled me," was Mary's reply.

Margaret looked at Elizabeth and stated, "I am sorry, it will never happen again."

Elizabeth remarked, "No it will not. They will not be able to play together ever again." With that the neighbors were gone.

* * * * *

There were other children about her age around, but their parents would not let them around Mary. Especially after what had happened to Madelyn.

She bit everyone.

Her mother started teaching her how to cook, shop for food, clean house, and sew, and all other womanly tasks. Mary would not have any of that. As soon as Margaret tried to teach her something, Mary would turn around and bite her mother.

As the girl grew older, she would follow her father to the docks to take the fish to the building to be preserved. She thought that was interesting, but she got bored quickly.

By this time she was a beautiful young woman. She no longer bit people. She was beginning to think more like a woman. She was especially interested in men. Mary would follow men around until they decided this girl was someone they could have their way with. They would follow her around until they could ask her to go with them.

She was soon called a prostitute. Having sex for money satisfied her for some time. She became quite wealthy. She never had to worry about where the next money was coming from. There were always men around at the dock. She was quite alluring.

Her father and mother were embarrassed. They ended up asking Mary to leave.

Mary did not think that was a problem. There were men everywhere she went. She could not understand why her parents were so against her. She was not doing anything wrong.

Part of the reason for the identification of Mary Magdalen as a sinner may derive from the reputation of her birthplace, Magdala, which by the late first century, was infamous for its inhabitants' alleged vice and licentiousness.

The information about the city of Magdala was from the internet.

Fresco is a mural painting that involves painting with water-based paint directly onto wet plaster so that the paint becomes an integral part of the plaster.

I studied a lot about Mary Magdalen. Nothing was said about her young years. Consequently I made up what I hadn't been able to research.

I invented the story about her being a crying baby and then a biter I had read that she was supposed to have been a prostitute, so I tried to make up what might have led to that profession. Anything I read said she was beautiful. So I thought that was a way I could incorporate her beauty and being alluring into the story.

Chapter Two
SEVEN EVIL SPIRITS

Mary was visiting her parents one day and she asked, "Mother, have you heard of Jesus of Nazareth?"

"No, who is he?"

"I think he is a prophet or something. I am hoping he can get rid of my Evil Spirits", Mary said.

Margaret stated, "I do not think anyone can."

"I think it is worth a try."

Mary had been to the Rabbi many times. She even consulted with Wizards to no avail. She was beginning to feel she would have those demons with her forever. They have tormented her since she was born.

* * * * *

Mary walked up slowly to the Messiah, "Lord, will you help me? I have been tormented by evil spirits since I was born."

She bowed her head because she was ashamed. She did not feel worthy of his healing powers.

"I have watched you heal others many times. I have been to Rabbis, Sooth Sayers and Wizards. No one has been able to help me. These evil spirits have made me do things I know that are wrong."

"We know who you are, Jesus of Nazareth. Lord, leave us alone," said the evil spirits.

Mary's countenance changed. The beautiful woman was racked with pain as the evil spirits tormented her.

The Master looked up and commanded, "Evil spirits come out of her and never return."

Mary quickly fell on her knees and kissed Jesus's feet until they were wet from her tears.

He lifted her up and looked into her eyes and said, "Go, my child, you have been cleansed and sin no more."

* * * * *

Mary immediately ran to her home. As she entered, she violently grabbed her mother, and gave her a big squeeze. Then she did the same to her father.

Then she stated, "I went to see Jesus of Nazareth. He sent all of my evil spirits out of me. Mother and Father, I love you. I am so sorry for all of the anguish I have put you through. I am healed and I have no more disposition to do that which is not right. Now all I want to do is follow Jesus wherever he goes. I want to watch him. He is so amazing."

"He must be amazing if he has rid you of all of your demons," Thomas said.

* * * * *

Thomas told everyone he saw about the miracle Jesus of Nazareth performed on his daughter.

From that day, Mary had no disposition to do anything she should not.

* * * * *

Soon afterwards, Jesus went on through cities and villages, proclaiming and bringing the good news of the kingdom of God. The twelve were with him, as well as some women who had been cured of evil spirits and infirmities. Besides Mary, Joanna, the wife of Herod's steward Chuza, and Susanna, and many others, followed Jesus. Mary Magdalen was seen as the most important of all of them.

All she could think about was being one of Jesus's disciples and following him everywhere he traveled. She knew it would mean a lot of walking, but she did not mind.

* * * * *

Jesus taught the people for three days without any food. They were all getting hungry and did not want to leave, because they were afraid they might miss something being taught.

Jesus said, "I feel bad, because these people have stayed with me for three days, and have had nothing to eat. I will not send them away fasting, lest they faint in the way.

And his disciples said, "Where can we go in the wilderness to get enough bread to fill so great a multitude?"

Jesus asked, "How many loaves do you have?"

They said, "Seven, and a few little fishes."

He commanded the multitude to sit on the ground. And he took the seven loaves and the fishes, and gave thanks, and broke them in pieces, and gave them to his disciples, and the disciples gave them in a basket to the multitude. Mary Magdalen had joined them.

And they did all eat, and were filled. And they took up of the broken bits of food, seven baskets full which was left.

And they that did eat were four thousand men, beside women and children.

And he sent the multitude away and got into a ship and came into the coasts of Magdala.

* * * * *

When he reached the shore there were many waiting for him with their sick and afflicted.

Also there, were Thomas and Margaret, Mary's parents. They were eager to thank Jesus for giving life to their daughter. She had suffered many years with the evil spirits.

"Thank you so much", Thomas said, "For sending all of the evil spirits out of Mary."

Margaret smiled, "I wish that could have been done many years before. She was tormented and so were we and many other people in our community. Now she is the daughter we can be proud of. We have always loved her even with all of her infirmities. However, we had many problems living with her ailments. Thank you again."

Jesus smiled and said, "Shalom."

Mary Magdalen hung her head and slowly walked to him.

He asked her, "What is your ailment?"

He said, "Yes, I did. I am glad to see that you have joined us. I also just met your father and mother."

She took his hands in hers and kissed them in gratitude for the spirits having left her. She felt better than she had at any time in her life. She had no desire to sin. All she wanted to do was to become a follower.

* * * * *

Mary Magdalen rushed back to the ship. He was not there. She stopped many people and asked, "Where is my Lord?"

One woman said, "He went back to the other side of the Sea."

Another said, "He has gone to be with his friends."

A man said, "He is healing some people in Cana."

Mary did not know which direction to go. Then she saw some people going toward the ship, she followed. On the other side of the Sea, much people gathered to him.

This story was related by one of his disciples:

"Jesus had gone to a mountain to pray. When he came down, he went to the Sea and saw that the men were having trouble keeping the ship afloat. He thought he had better go to them. He started walking on the water. When the men in the ship saw him walking on the water, they were afraid. They thought he was a ghost. Then he called out to them, 'Be of good cheer. It is I, be not afraid.'

"And he went up into the ship and the wind ceased and all was calm. Soon they were on the other side of the Sea."

The people, including Mary Magdalen, were waiting for him. When the disciple related the story, all were amazed.

One man said, "What manner of man is this? Even the winds and the sea obey him."

All Mary Magdalen could say, "He can do all things. He is wonderful."

And when he came to the other side, into the country of the Gergesenes, he met two men possessed with devils, coming out of the tombs, exceedingly fierce, so that no man might pass by that way.

And they cried out saying, "What have we to do with you, Jesus, the Son of God? Have you come to torment us before our time?

And there was a good way off from them a herd of many swine feeding.

So the devils asked him, "If you cast us out, let us go away into the herd of swine."

And he said, to them, "Go". And when they came out of the two men, they went into the swine. And the whole herd of swine ran violently down a steep place into the sea, and perished in the water.

And they that took care of the swine, fled and went their way into the city, and told everything that happened to the men possessed of the devils.

Mary Magdalen marveled at the fact that Jesus could transport the evil spirits into the swine. She smiled. She would have him for her own someday.

* * * * *

And behold, the whole city came out to meet Jesus and when they saw him, they asked him to depart out of their coasts.

* * * * *

And there came one of the rulers of the Synagogue. His name was Jarius; and when he saw him, he fell at his feet, and spoke to him saying, "My little daughter lies at the point of death: I pray, come and lay your hands on her, that she may be healed; she will live.

And Jesus went with him; and a lot of people followed him including Mary Magdalen. She was anxious to see what he would do.

Instead of going to the girl he was weary because there were so many people walking so close to him that he was having trouble going with the ruler of the Synagogue.

A certain woman, which had a blood disease for twelve years and had suffered many things of many physicians, and had spent all that she had, and was not any better, but rather grew worse. When she had heard of Jesus, she came behind him. All she did was touch the hem of his garment.

For she said, "If I may touch but his clothes, I will be healed."

And Jesus, immediately knowing that some of his strength had gone out of him, turned himself around and said, "Who touched my clothes?"

He looked and saw her.

But the woman fearing and trembling, knowing what had been done, came and fell down before him, and told him it was she that had touched him.

And he said to her, "Daughter, your faith has made you well. Go in peace, and be rid of your plague."

* * * * *

A man came from the ruler of the Synagogue's house which said, "Your daughter is dead. Do not trouble the Master any further."

When Jesus heard that, he said, "Be not afraid, only believe."

He did not want anyone to follow him except Peter, and James and John.

He did not know that Mary Magdalen followed a pace behind.

And he came to the house of the ruler of the Synagogue, and seeing the tumult, and them that wept and wailed extremely.

And he said, "Why do you weep? The damsel is not dead, but sleeps.

They laughed at him. But when he had put them all out, he took the father and the mother and those he chose to go with him, into the room where the damsel was lying.

When the mourners retreated from the house, Mary Magdalen asked, "Why were you sent out and why are you laughing?"

"That man said the girl was not dead. We laughed because we knew she was dead. That is why we were there."

Then he took the damsel by the hand, and said to her, "arise."

Everyone was astonished. And Jesus said to give her something to eat.

* * * * *

When he came out of the house he noticed that Mary Magdalen was with some other women. He looked at her and smiled.

She got chills all over her body. She said to herself, (He recognized me.) She was thrilled.

But he had so much work to do.

Two blind men followed him, saying, "Son of David, have mercy on us."

And when Jesus went into a house, the blind men came to him. And Jesus said to them, "Do you believe that I am able to do this?" They said, "Yes, Lord".

Then he touched their eyes, saying, "According to your faith be healed."

Then their eyes were opened.

Mary Magdalen was so excited. She was seeing him perform miracles.

* * * * *

Jesus noticed that the beautiful woman he had cleanse of the seven evil spirits was with the group of woman that were following him.

Mary Magdalen pushed her way closer, so she could see and hear better. The other women wanted to get closer, too, but they were not aggressive enough.

The woman was beginning to have strong feelings for the Messiah. If Jesus had feelings other than knowing he had healed her, he had to keep it to himself. He was doing the work God had given him to do.

* * * * *

People watched for Jesus. When they saw him coming, they would bring those whom they wanted him to heal. One brought him a dumb man possessed with a devil.

When the devil was cast out, the dumb spoke. And the multitude marveled.

But the Pharisees said, "He casts out devils through the power of the devils.

* * * * *

Jesus went about all of the cities and villages, teaching in their Synagogues, and preaching the gospel of the Kingdom, and healing every sickness and every disease among the people.

Mary Magdalen listened intently to every word he spoke. All of the people listened, but she seemed to drink it all in.

Jesus walks on the water and calms the sea is found in the King James Bible Mark 6:45-52

Jesus feeds 4,000 plus women and children is found in the King James Bible, Matthew 15:32-39.

Jesus heals woman who touches his clothes is found in the King James Bible, Mark 5:25-34

Jesus casts demons into a herd of Swine is found in the King James Bible, Matthew 8:28-33

Jesus raises Jarius' Daughter Back to Life is found in the King James Bible Mark 5:21-24 and 35-43

Jesus heals two blind men is found in the King James Bible Matthew 9:27-31

Jesus heals a man unable to speak is found in the King James Bible Matthew 9:32-34

The fact that women played such an active and important role in Jesus's ministry was not entirely radical or even unique. Jesus's ministry did bring women greater liberation than they would have typically held in mainstream Jewish society.

Part of the reason for the identification of Mary Magdalen as a sinner may derive from the reputation of her birthplace, Magdala, which by the late first century, was infamous for its inhabitants alleged vice and licentiousness.

Chapter Three
MORE MIRACLES

M ary Magdalen loved to watch Jesus perform miracles. She knew he was the most wonderful man she had ever met. She stayed with the women so she would not look conspicuous. She did not want anyone to know that she loved him. And she was sure he loved her. She could tell. Every time he noticed that she was in the congregation, he made a point of smiling at her. She was not about to leave his presence unless he went alone with just his apostles.

Mary Hannah, Mary Magdalen's friend asked, "Would you like to go into Jerusalem with us?" There were about ten women in all. Mary Magdalen replied, "No, I think I will stay here. I enjoy watching Jesus perform the miracles."

Ruth said, "I know. You just want to stay close to Jesus."

Mary Magdalen whispered, "Can you blame me? He is sooo good looking and he does things that nobody has ever seen before. Of course, I want to stay near."

Mary Esther remarked, "Everyone knows how you feel. We want to see the city. Who knows, maybe we can find some good looking, eligible men. I am sure there are enough to go around." She put her hand over her mouth and giggled.

"You go ahead, and good luck", Mary Magdalen hung her head ashamedly. "I would rather stay here."

It turned out, she was the only woman left. The men, in the gathering, watched her intently. Her beauty was incomparable. She stood out in the crowd. Most of the men wanted to stand as close to her as possible, without being too obvious. She was unaware of the men who were crowding around her. She was totally focused on Jesus and his oratories.

Jesus was telling the group about repentance. He stated, "Without repentance no one can enter the kingdom of Heaven. Nobody is perfect. You need to repent every day. You should ask God to forgive you even for the small things you do wrong."

A man spoke up, "What kind of things do we ask for forgiveness from?"

"Only you know what you do that is wrong," Jesus answered. "Some things are idle gossiping."

"Sometimes you say small things that are hurtful and you are unaware of the consequences. There are always consequences when someone's feelings are hurt. If you know you have hurt someone else's feelings, you should go to that person and ask forgiveness."

"If someone comes to you and says you have hurt his feelings, you should apologize immediately and try not to make that same mistake again. In the end, you may have gained a good friend."

"If he does not accept your apology, then you have done your best. He may not have been your friend in the first place. Remember, if you forgive someone, then your Heavenly Father will forgive you. However, if you will not forgive a person, you cannot expect Heavenly Father to forgive you of your trespasses."

"How, do you know if God has forgiven you?" A man asked.

"You may not know right away, but by and by you will feel that you have been forgiven because you will feel happier," Jesus commented.

Mary Magdalen asked, "What if you know you have done something terrible, but you have done your best to repent?"

"Heavenly Father looks on the heart. Repentance is knowing you have done something wrong and are changing. You must feel sorrow and never do it again. Then you should try to forget it. If you have truly repented, God will forgive you and he will remember it no more."

"That sounds wonderful, but when will you know that you have been forgiven?" Mary Magdalen said.

Jesus answered, "When you have no disposition to repeat the act."

Mary Magdalen was satisfied with Jesus's answer. She hoped that someday she would feel God's love for her. As yet she did not feel she had been forgiven for her sins, but she was still trying.

* * * * *

Jesus was teaching in one of the Synagogues on the Sabbath.

And, behold, there was a woman which had a spirit of infirmity eighteen years, and was bowed together, and could in no wise lift herself up.

And when Jesus saw her, he called her to him, and said to her, "Woman, you are loosed from your infirmity."

And he laid his hands on her, and immediately she was made straight, and she glorified God.

And the ruler of the synagogue answered with indignation, because Jesus had healed on the Sabbath, and said to the people, "There are six days in which men ought to work, therefore come and be healed, and not on the Sabbath."

The Lord then answered him, and said, "You hypocrite, does not each one of you on the Sabbath loose his ox or his ass from the stall, and lead him away to be watered? And should not this woman, being a daughter of Abraham, whom Satan has bound these eighteen years, be loosed from this bond on the Sabbath?"

And when he had said these things, all his adversaries were ashamed, and all the people rejoiced for all the glorious things that were done by him.

* * * * *

After this there was a feast of the Jews; and Jesus went into the city of Jerusalem. He sent two of his disciples saying, "Go into the village over against you, and straightway you shall find an ass tied, and a colt with her. Loose them, and bring them to me.

"And if any man say ought unto you, you shall say, 'The Lord hath need of them,' and straightway he will send them."

All this was done, that it might be fulfilled which was spoken by the prophet, saying, "Tell ye the daughter of Sion, 'Behold, thy King cometh unto thee, meek, and sitting upon an ass, and a colt the foal of an ass.'"

And the disciples went, and did as Jesus commanded them, and brought the ass, and the colt, and put on them their clothes, and they set him on it.

And the multitudes that went before, and that followed, cried, saying, "Hosanna to the Son of David. Blessed is he that cometh in the name of the Lord, Hosanna in the highest."

And when he was come into Jerusalem, all the city was moved, saying, "Who is this?"

And the multitude said, "This is Jesus the prophet of Nazareth of Galilee."

Mary Magdalen and her friends were watching as this all took place. She marveled, "How meek Jesus is to enter Jerusalem sitting on an ass. He is a King. He should have come in regal clothes in a fine chariot."

Her friend asked, "Who told you he is a King?"

"No one had to tell me, I just know," She sobbed.

* * * * *

And Jesus went into the temple of God, and cast out all them that sold and bought in the temple, and overthrew the tables of the moneychangers, and the seat of them that sold doves, and said to them, "It is written, My house shall be called the house of prayer, but you have made it a den of thieves.

And the blind and the lame came to him in the temple, and he healed them.

And when the chief priests and scribes saw the wonderful things that he did, and the children crying in the temple, and saying, "Hosanna to the Son of David," they were very displeased.

And they said to him, "Do you hear what the children are saying?" And Jesus said to them, "Yes, have you never read, Out of the mouth of babes and suckling's you have perfected praise?"

Mary Magdalen smiled when she heard Jesus reprimanding the authorities.

* * * * *

Now there is at Jerusalem by the sheep market a pool, which is called Bethesda, having five porches.

In these lay a great multitude of impotent folk, of blind, halt, and withered, waiting for the moving of the water.

For an angel went down at a certain season into the pool, made the water move. Whosoever the first one to step in was made well of whatsoever disease he had.

A certain man was there, which had an infirmity thirty and eight years.

When Jesus saw him lie, and knew that he had been now a long time there. He said to him, "Would you like to be made well?"

The impotent man answered him, "Sir I have no man, when the water is moving, to put me into the pool, but while I am coming, another steps down before me."

Mary Magdalen watched carefully. (Was he going to set him in the water? What would he do next?)

Jesus said to him, "Rise, take up your bed, and walk."

(What? That was all?) Mary Magdalen was perplexed.

And immediately the man was healed, and took up his bed and walked.

(That was magnificent. Who knew that all Jesus had to say was, 'Pick up your bed and walk?')

And Jesus did this on the Sabbath.

The Jews therefore said to the man that was healed, "It is not lawful for you to carry your bed on the Sabbath.

He answered them, "He that healed me, said to me, 'Take up your bed and walk.'"

And he that was healed did not know who it was: for Jesus had gone away.

Afterward Jesus saw him in the temple, and said to him, "Behold, you are healed. Sin no more, or a worse thing will happen to you."

The man left, and told the Jews that it was Jesus, who had healed him.

And therefore did the Jews persecute Jesus and sought to kill him, because he had done it on the Sabbath.

Mary Magdalen watched from afar. She could not understand why Jesus was not supposed to heal people on the Sabbath. (Why make the man wait until the next day. I think it is important to heal a man or woman when he finds one who ails.)

* * * * *

Then he went by ship into a desert place. The people followed him on foot.

Mary Magdalen never seems to tire watching Jesus perform the miracles. She felt she would walk to the ends of the earth to see him heal.

And Jesus saw a great multitude, and he had compassion toward them, and he healed their sick.

And when it was evening, his disciples came to him, saying, "This is a desert place, and the time is now past. Send the multitude away, that they may go into the villages, and buy themselves food."

But Jesus said to them, "They do not need to leave, give them food to eat."

And they said to him, "We have five loaves and two fishes."

He said, "Bring them here to me."

And he commanded the multitude to sit down on the grass, and took the five loaves and the two fishes, and looking up to heaven, he blessed, and broke the offerings and gave the loaves to his disciples, and the disciples gave it to the multitude.

And they all ate, and were filled. And they took up the fragments that remained twelve baskets full.

And they that had eaten were about five thousand men, beside women and children.

Mary Magdalen said to her friends, "He is amazing." Then she thought to herself, (I think he is the Messiah. Nobody else could take a few loaves of bread and a few fish and feed five thousand men and also women and children. Yes, he has to be God's Only Begotten Son. I had heard about him, but so has many others. Do they feel the way I do?)

* * * * *

(It is amazing how many people Jesus heals and he never turns anyone away.) Mary Magdalen thought to herself.

Jesus overlooked the crowd. He could not believe that many people would follow him, no matter where he went. Most of them he recognized. They seemed to be devout disciples. He smiled at the congregation. Mary Magdalen thought he only smiled at her.

Mary Magdalen felt he had smiled at her especially. She got chills thinking about it. She loved him so much.

Then Jesus departed into the coasts of Tyre and Sidon.

And behold, a woman of Canaan came out of the same coasts, and cried unto him, saying, "Have mercy on me, O Lord, Son of David. My daughter is grievously vexed with a devil.

But he did not say anything. His disciples came and asked, "Send her away; for she cries after us."

But he said, "I am not sent but to the lost sheep of the house of Israel."

Then she came and worshipped him, saying, "Lord, help me."

But he answered and said, "It is not right to take the children's bread and to give it to the dogs."

And she said, "That is true Lord, yet the dogs eat of the crumbs which fall from their masters table."

Then Jesus said, "O woman, great is your faith." And her daughter was healed from that very hour.

Jesus rides triumph in to Jerusalem riding on an ass is found in the New Testament King James Matt21:1-11

Jesus cleanses the temple is found in the New Testament King James Matt 21:12-16

Jesus heals a woman who had been crippled eighteen years is found in the New Testament King James Luke 13:10-17

Jesus heals an invalid at Bethesda is found in the New Testament King James Luke 5:1-15

Jesus feeds five thousand is found in the New Testament King James Matt 14:13-21

Jesus heals gentile woman's demon possessed daughter is found in the New Testament Matt 15:21-28

Chapter Four
JESUS CONTINUES TEACHING

J esus went up into a mountain, and sat down there.

And great multitudes came to him bringing those who were lame, blind, dumb, maimed, and many others, and brought them one by one to the feet of Jesus, and he healed them.

Because of that, the multitude wondered, when they saw the dumb to speak, the maimed to be healed, the lame to walk, and the blind to see, they glorified the God of Israel.

Mary Magdalen continued to follow him wherever he went. By this time she was convinced that Jesus was the long awaited Messiah. She also knew that he was hers alone.

* * * * *

As Jesus and the multitude were walking, he saw a man which was blind from his birth.

And his disciples asked him, saying, "Master, who did sin, this man, or his parents, that he was born blind?"

Jesus answered, "Neither hath this man sinned, nor his parents. But that the works of God should be made manifest in him. I must work the works of him that sent me, while it is day: the night comes, when no man can work. As long as I am in the world, I am the light of the world.

When he had said this, he spat on the ground and made clay of the spittle, and he anointed the eyes of the blind man with the clay.

And he said to him, "Go, and wash in the pool of Siloam. The man went and washed and was able to see.

The neighbors and they which had seen him before said, "Is this the man who sat and begged?"

Some said, "This is he." Others said, "He is like him." But the man said, "I am he."

Then they said to him, "How were your eyes opened?"

He answered and said, "A man that is called Jesus made clay, and anointed my eyes, and said to me, 'Go to the pool of Siloam, and wash,' and I went and washed and I received sight"

Then they said to him, "Where is he?"

He said, "I know not."

Mary Magdalen looked around, (Where could he have gone? He was just here. I was watching him.)

* * * * *

The men took him that had been blind to the Pharisees. And it was the Sabbath day when Jesus made the clay, and opened his eyes.

Then the Pharisees also asked him how he had received his sight. He said to them, "He put clay on my eyes, and I washed, and do see.

The Pharisees said, "This man is not of God, because he does not keep the Sabbath day."

Others said, "How can a sinner do such miracles?" And there was a division among them.

They said to the blind man again, "What do you say of him that has opened your eyes?"

He said, "He is a prophet."

But the Jews did not believe him, that he had been blind, and received his sight, until they called the parents of him that had been blind.

And they asked them, "Is this your son, who you say was born blind? How then does he now see?"

His parents answered and said, "We know that this is our son, and that he was born blind, but by what means he can now see, or who opened his eyes, we do not know. He is of age, ask him, he can speak for himself."

Then again they called the man and said to him, "Give God the praise, we know this man is a sinner."

He answered and said, "Whether he is a sinner or no, I do not know. One thing I know, I was blind and now I see."

Then they said again, "What did he do to you? How did he open your eyes?"

He answered, "I have told you already and you did not hear. Why would you hear it again? Will you also be his disciples?"

"We know that God spoke to Moses. As for this fellow, we do not know where he is from."

The man answered and said, "Why is it that he has done this marvelous thing and you do not know where he is from? Yet he has opened my eyes.

Now we know that God does not hear sinners, but if any man be a worshipper of God, and does his will, he will hear him. Since the world began, was it heard that any man opened the eyes of any man that was born blind? If this man were not of God, he could do nothing."

Mary Magdalen knew that the man spoke the truth. She was impressed by the miracle that had been done for the blind man. She knew the truth about Jesus and she was sure the man did too.

* * * * *

Where was Jesus? He had not been seen since he healed the blind man. His disciples had gone, too.

Mary Magdalen started to panic. She must find Jesus. She did not want to miss out on any of his miracles.

She asked the women she had been with. They had not seen him leave, but they pointed the way that the disciples had gone.

She hurried in that direction.

* * * * *

Some tension occurred because of Mary Magdalen's closeness to Jesus. Peter was jealous because she is a woman and of special teaching given to her.

The disciples were following Jesus. They were near the town of Bethany.

Mary Magdalen was familiar with Bethany. That was where Mary, Martha, and Lazarus lived. She had been there when Mary anointed Jesus with ointment and wiped his feet with her hair. He loved them. They loved him.

Martha had become upset because Mary would not help her fix dinner. Jesus had told her that Mary had chosen the best.

The sisters sent for him, saying, "Lord, behold, Lazarus is sick."

When Jesus heard that, he said, "This sickness will not be for his death, but for the glory of God, that the Son of God might be glorified by Him."

When he had heard that Lazarus was sick, he stayed two days yet in the same place where he was.

Then after that he said to his disciples said, "Let us go into Judea again."

His disciples said to him, "Master, the Jews want to stone you, and you want to go there again?"

Jesus answered, "Our friend Lazarus sleeps, but I go, that I may awake him out of his sleep."

Then his disciples said, Lord, if he sleeps, he will do well."

However, Jesus spoke of his death. They thought that he had spoken of him resting.

Then Jesus said to them plainly, "Lazarus is dead."

Mary Magdalen was standing close enough that she could hear all that was said. (She wondered, if he is sleeping, how can he be dead? Or if he is dead, why did Jesus say he was sleeping?)

She and the other women who were standing nearby, listened carefully so they could understand what was happening.

Then Jesus continued, "I am glad for your sakes that I was not there, so you may believe. Nevertheless, we will go to him now.

Then when Jesus came, he found that he had lain in the grave four days already.

Now Bethany was not too far from Jerusalem.

Many of the Jews came to Martha and Mary, to comfort them concerning their brother.

When Martha heard that Jesus was coming, she went and met him, but Mary still sat in the house.

Mary Magdalen put her arm around Martha's shoulder for comfort.

Then Martha said to Jesus, "Lord, if you had been here, my brother would not have died. But I know, that even now, whatsoever you will ask God, He will give it to you."

Jesus said, "Your brother will rise again."

Martha replied, "I know that he will rise again in the resurrection at the last day."

Jesus said to her, "I am the resurrection and the life. He that believes in me, though he were dead, yet will he live. And who lives and believes in me will never die. Do you believe this?"

She said to him, "Yea, Lord. I believe that you are the Christ, the Son of God, which has come into the world."

And when she had said this, she went and called Mary saying, "The Master has come and he calls for you."

As soon as she heard that, Mary arose quickly and came to him.

Jesus had not come into the town of Bethany, but was in the place where Martha met him.

The Jews that were in the house with Mary to comfort her, saw that she rose up fast and went out, followed her saying, "She is going to the grave to weep there."

When Mary had come to the place where Jesus was, she fell down at his feet, saying, "Lord if you had been here, my brother would not have died."

When Jesus saw her crying, and the Jews also weeping, he groaned, and was troubled.

And he said, "Where have you laid him?"

They said to him, "Lord, come and see."

Jesus wept.

Mary Magdalen, seeing Jesus weep, wept also.

Then the Jews said, "Behold how he loved him!"

And some of them said, "Could not this man, which opened the eyes of the blind, have caused that even this man should not have died?"

Jesus again groaning came to the grave. It was a cave, and a stone lay on it.

Jesus said, "Take away the stone."

Martha, the sister of him that was dead, said to him, "Lord, by this time he stinks, for he has been dead four days."

Jesus said to her, "Said I not to you, that if you would believe, you will see the glory of God?"

They took away the stone from the cave.

And Jesus lifted up his eyes, and said, "Father, I thank you that you have heard me. And I knew that you hear me always, but because of the people which stand by, I said it, that they may believe that you have sent me."

And when he had spoken, he cried with a loud voice, "Lazarus, come forth."

And Lazarus came from the cave, bound hand and foot with grave clothes, and his face was bound about with a napkin. Jesus said to them, "Loose him, and let him go."

Mary Magdalen was mesmerized, as were the women she was with.

Then many of the Jews which came to Mary, and had seen the things which Jesus did, believed on him.

But some of them went their way to the Pharisees, and told them what things Jesus had done.

* * * * *

Then the chief priests and the Pharisees gathered in a council, and said, "What should we do? For this man does many miracles. If we let him alone, all men will believe him, and the Romans will come and take away both our place and nation."

And one of them, named Caiaphas, being the high priest that same year, said, "You know nothing at all, nor consider that it is expedient for us, that one man should die for the people, and that the whole nation will not parish."

And he spoke not of himself, but being high priest that year, he prophesied that Jesus should die for the nation. And not for the nation only, but that also he should gather together in one the children of God that were scattered abroad.

Then from that day they took counsel together to put Jesus to death.

* * * * *

From that time Jesus was not seen openly, but went into a country near the wilderness, into a city called Ephraim. His disciples resorted there also.

Jesus healed a man blind from birth is found in the New Testament King James John 9:1-33

Jesus raises Lazarus from the dead is found in the New Testament King James John 11:1-46

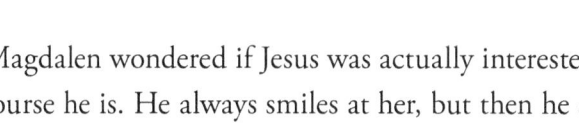

Chapter Five
FOLLOWING
THE SAVIOR

Mary Magdalen wondered if Jesus was actually interested in her. Of course he is. He always smiles at her, but then he smiles at everyone. Why did she think she was a special disciple? Yes, she was a disciple. She followed Him wherever he went. So did hundreds of other disciples. Was she wasting her time? Of course not. She was learning things she never felt she would ever have known, otherwise.

She had given up and repented of her old profession. If it had not been for Jesus, she would not know that repentance was possible.

She had also learned the meaning of unconditional love. That was a difficult precept, but one she would have to work on for the rest of her life.

He had taught the Ten Commandments. Her parents had taught them to her when she was young, but because of the evil spirits that she had within her, she did not understand them and did not want to.

She had given her parents a hard time. She did not want to do anything they tried to teach her. She was so obstinate. Nothing mattered but her so called pleasure.

Pleasure! That was pleasure? No, she did not know the meaning of pleasure until she started learning from the Savior. He taught her things she never would have learned. Not only her, but all of his disciples or followers.

* * * * *

(I am following Him again, along with the other women disciples.)

* * * * *

When Jesus came out, it was evening and he said to his twelve disciples, "Let us go to the other side of the sea."

Again, Mary Magdalen was not invited, so she entered into one of the smaller boats to get to the other side of the sea.

And when they had sent away the multitude, they took him in the ship. And there were also with him other little ships.

And there arose a great storm of wind, and the waves beat into the ship, so that it was now full.

And Jesus was in the back part of the ship, asleep on a pillow. And they woke him, and said to him, "Master, do you not care that we perish?"

And he arose, and rebuked the wind and said to the sea, "Peace, be still." And the wind ceased, and there was a great calm.

And he said to them, "Why are you so fearful? How is it that you have no faith?"

And they were exceedingly afraid, and said to one another, "What manner of man is this, that even the wind and the sea obey him?"

* * * * *

And immediately, his fame spread abroad throughout all the region round about Galilee.

And when they came out of the Synagogue, they entered into the house of Simon and Andrew, with James and John.

Simon's wife's mother lay sick of a fever, and right away they told Jesus of her.

And Jesus came and took her by the hand, and lifted her up, and immediately the fever left her, and she served them.

And at evening, when the sun did set, they brought to him all that were diseased, and them that were possessed with devils.

And all the city was gathered together at the door.

And he healed many that were sick of diverse diseases, and cast out many devils and suffered not the devils to speak, because they knew him.

* * * * *

And there came a leper to him, begging and kneeling down to him, and saying, "You can make me clean."

And Jesus said to him, "I will. Be clean."

And as soon as he had spoken, immediately the leprosy departed from him, and he was cleansed.

All of this time, Mary Magdalen was watching and learning from the Master. She did not want to miss anything.

* * * * *

Jesus entered in Capernaum.

And a certain centurion's servant, who was dear to him, was sick, and ready to die.

And when he heard of Jesus, he sent to him the elders of the Jews, begging him that he would come and heal his servant.

And when they came to Jesus, they begged him instantly, saying, "He was worthy for whom he should do this. For he loves our nation, and he has built us a Synagogue.

Then Jesus went with them. And when he was now not far from the house, the centurion sent friends to him, saying to him, "Lord, trouble not yourself, for I am not worthy that you should enter under my roof. Wherefore neither I thought myself worthy to come to you, but say in a word, and my servant shall be healed. For I am a man set under authority, having under me soldiers, and I say to one, 'Go, and he goes,' and to another, 'Come and he comes', and to my servant, 'Do this, and he does it.'

When Jesus heard these things, he marveled at him, and turned him about, and said to the people that followed him, "I say to you, I have not found so great faith, no not in Israel."

And they that were sent, returning to the house, found the servant well that had been sick.

* * * * *

And it came to pass also on another Sabbath, he entered in the synagogue and taught. And there was a man whose right hand was withered.

And the scribes and Pharisees watched him, whether he would heal on the Sabbath, that they might find an accusation against him.

But he knew their thoughts, and said to the man which had the withered hand, "Rise up, and stand forth in the midst." And he arose and stood forth.

Then Jesus said to them, "I will ask you one thing. Is it lawful on the Sabbath to do good, or to do evil? To save life, or to destroy it?"

And looking round about on them all, he said to the man, "Stretch forth your hand." And he did so, and his hand was restored like the other.

And they were filled with madness. And communed one with another what they might do to Jesus.

Jesus calms a storm on the sea is found in the New Testament in Mark 4:35-41

Jesus healed Peter's mother-in-law is found in the New Testament in Mark 1:29-31

Jesus heals a man with leprosy is found in the New Testament in Mark1:40-45

Jesus heals a Centurian's, paralyzed servant in Capernaum is found in the New Testament in Luke 7:1-10

Jesus heals a mans withered hand on the Sabbath is found in the New Testament in Luke 6:6-11

Chapter Six
STILL FOLLOWING

Mary Magdalen was still following her mentor. He had taught her so much, she could not absorb it all. She figured, if she continued being his shadow she had to remember most of what she heard.

(His teaching is wonderful, but most of all, I love the way he heals the people.)

And how he loves everyone with unconditional love. I do not understand how it is possible to love every person no matter what they had done. Even me! I had lived a life of sin. I know I was racked with torment from seven evil spirits. He cast the spirits out from me. Nobody can understand that one person can have seven evil spirits in one body. Seven of them! It was no wonder that I had done bad things since the day I was born.

My saintly mother put up with more than any mother should have to. I guess you could say she loved unconditionally, and still does. Being a mother, instills a love that nobody can explain. I have never been a mother, therefore, I cannot feel a mother's love. All I know, is that God gives mothers special gifts to help them through raising children.)

* * * * *

When Jesus came to his disciples, he saw a great multitude about them, and the scribes questioning them.

And straightway all the people, when they saw him, were greatly amazed, and they ran to him and saluted him.

And he asked the scribes, "What are you questioning them about?"

And one of the multitude answered and said, "Master, I have brought my son to you which has a dumb spirit."

Mary Magdalen could sympathize with the boy, but he should be happy he only has one dumb spirit. (I carried seven evil spirits around for about twenty years.)

The father continued, "Wherever I take him, the spirit tares him. And he foams, and gnashes with his teeth, and pines away. And I spoke to your disciples and they could not cast him out."

He answered him, and said, "Oh faithless generation, how long will I be with you? Bring him to me."

And they brought him to Jesus, and when he saw him, right away the spirit tore him. And he fell on the ground, and wallowed foaming.

And he asked his father, "How long has this been happening?"

And he said, "Since he was a child. Sometimes it has cast him into the fire, and also into the water, to destroy him, but if you can do anything, have compassion on us, and help us."

Jesus said to him, "If you can believe, all things are possible to him that believes."

And right away the father of the child cried out, and said with tears, "Lord, I believe, help my unbelief."

When Jesus saw that the people came running together, he rebuked the four spirits, saying to him, "You dumb and deaf spirit, I charge you, come out of him, and enter into him no more."

And the spirit cried, and tore him. And the people thought he was dead.

But Jesus took him by the hand, and lifted him up, and he arose.

Mary Magdalen marveled at the miracle performed by Jesus. It brought back fond memories.

And when he came in the house, his disciple asked him privately, "Why were we not able to cast them out?"

And he said to them, "This kind can only come out by prayer and fasting."

* * * * *

And they went to Capernaum, and right away. On the Sabbath day he entered into the Synagogue, and taught. And they were astonished at his doctrine. For he taught them as one that had authority, and not as the scribes.

And there was in their Synagogue a man with an unclean spirit; and he cried out, saying, "Let us alone, what have we to do with you, Jesus of Nazareth? Have you come to destroy us? I know who you are, the Holy One of God."

And Jesus rebuked him, saying, "Hold your peace, and come out of him."

And when the unclean spirit had torn the man, and cried with a loud voice, he came out of him.

And they were all amazed, insomuch that they questioned among themselves, saying, "What thing is this? What new doctrine is this? For with authority he commands even the unclean spirits, and they obey him."

And immediately his fame spread throughout all the region round about Galilee.

Mary Magdalen was not surprised. She had seen the Master perform so many miracles that not much surprised her.

* * * * *

When they came to the Sea of Galilee, the people brought a man that was deaf, and had an impediment in his speech. And they begged him to put his hand on him.

And he took him aside from the multitude, and put his fingers in his ears, and he spit, and touched his tongue.

And looking up to heaven, he sighed, and said to him, "Be opened."

And right away his ears were opened, and the string of his tongue was loosed, and he spoke plain.

And he charged them that they should tell no man. But the more he charged them, so it was told much more.

And everyone was beyond measure astonished, saying, "He has done all things great. He made both the deaf to hear, and the dumb to speak."

Mary Magdalen was not surprised. She had seen a multitude of miracles done by the Savior.

* * * * *

And he was casting out a devil, and it was dumb. And when the devil was gone, the dumb spoke, and the people wondered.

But some of them said, "He casts the devils out through Beelzebub, the chief of the devils."

And others, tempting him, wanted to see a sign from heaven.

But he, knowing their thoughts, said to them, "Every kingdom divided against itself is brought to desolation, and a house divided against a house falls."

"If Satan is divided against himself, how will his kingdom stand? Because you say that I cast out devils through Beelzebub. And if I by Beelzebub cast out devils, by whom do your sons cast them out? Therefore, will they be your judges."

"But if I with the finger of God cast out devils, no doubt the Kingdom of God is come upon you."

"When a strong man armed keeps his palace, his goods are in peace. But when a stronger man comes upon him, and overcomes him, he takes from him all his armor wherein he trusted, and divides the spoils."

"He that is not with me is against me. And he that gathers not with me scatters."

Mary Magdalen said to herself (I will always stay by his side and listen to him and obey all of his commandments.)

* * * * *

Mary Magdalen always felt she was one of Jesus's apostles, and the closest and most beloved disciple and the only one who truly understood his teachings.

(My closeness to Jesus results in a lot of tension with Peter. He always seems jealous of me because of the special teachings given to me. I consider myself to be the Apostle of the apostles.

I guess Jesus and all of the disciples called me Mary Magdalen because there are so many Mary's, it seemed like a good way of distinguishing between all of us. Most of the women I associated with were named Mary.)

* * * * *

And the companion of the Savior was Mary Magdalen. Christ loved Mary more than all the disciples, and used to kiss her often on the mouth. The rest of the disciples were offended by it and expressed disapproval. They said to him, "Why do you love her more than all of us?"

The Savior answered and said to them, "Why do I not love you like her? When a blind man and one who sees are both together in darkness, they are no different from one another. When the light comes, then he who sees will see the light, and he who is blind will remain in darkness."

* * * * *

And as he went to Jerusalem, that he passed through the middle of Samaria and Galilee.

And as he entered into a certain village, he met ten men that were lepers, which stood off a ways.

And they lifted up their voices, and said, "Jesus, Master, have mercy on us."

And when he saw them, he said to them, "Go show yourselves to the priests." And as they went, they were cleansed.

And one of them, when he saw that he was healed, turned back, and with a loud voice glorified God.

And fell down on his face at his feet, giving him thanks, and he was a Samaritan.

And Jesus answering said, "Were there not ten cleansed? But where are the nine? There are not found that returned to give glory to God, except this stranger."

And he said to him, "Arise, go your way. Your faith has healed you."

Mary Magdalen just smiled, (Another act of unconditional love.)

* * * * *

Judas Iscariot, went to the chief priests, and said to them, "What will you give to me, and I will deliver Jesus to you?"

And they said to him, "for thirty pieces of silver."

* * * * *

(I feel unusual that I have been seen as the most important out of all the woman disciples. The only explanation I can give is because I was with Jesus when none of the other women were.)

_____

Jesus heals an Official's son at Capernaum in Galilee is found in the New Testament in Mark 1:21-27

Jesus heals a deaf and dumb man is found in the New Testament in Mark 7:31-37

Jesus heals blind, mute demoniac is found in the New Testament in Luke 11:14-23

Jesus cleanses ten lepers on the way to Jerusalem is found in the New Testament in Luke 17:11-190

Judas plots with the chief priests is found in the New Testament in Matthew 26:14-16

In the Gospel of Philip there is a passage alluding to Jesus's relationship to Mary Magdalen.

For early Christians, Kissing did not have a romantic connotation and it was common for Christians to kiss their fellow believers as a way of greeting. In the context of Gospel of Philip, the kiss of peace is used as a symbol for the passage of truth from one person to another.

In 2016 Pope Francis called for her to be referred as the Apostle of the apostles. Other Protestant churches honor her as a heroine of the faith.

Chapter Seven
PASSOVER

It was time for the Passover.

Mary Magdalen was with the other women and did not know where Jesus and his disciples had gone. She was hoping to spend Passover with him, but he was nowhere to be found.

So she and her friends went to Jerusalem and celebrated Passover with them.

Mary Esther welcomed the women into their house for the celebration. Her husband, Lucius, officiated in the ceremony.

Mary Magdalen had trouble concentrating on the ritual. All she could think of was Jesus. Where was he? Was he having the Passover without her?

After the midnight part of the Passover, she left to see if she could find the Master. The rest of the women stayed at Lucius and Mary Esther's home to sleep.

Sleep? Mary Magdalen would not be able to sleep. She walked the streets of Jerusalem to no avail. The streets were empty. People had returned to their homes to sleep.

_____

Mary Magdalen's Passover experience was totally made up of my imagination.

Chapter Eight
JESUS'S TRIAL AND DEATH

Mary Magdalen heard soft talking. She walked in that direction. Just ahead of her she saw a small group of men walking over the brook Cedron, where there was a garden into which Jesus and his disciples entered. She walked softly so no one would hear her.

Then she heard a loud commotion. She looked to see one of Jesus's disciples. It was Judas Iscariot.

(What was he doing? There was a group of men and officers from the chief priests and Pharisees. They came with lanterns and torches.) She let out a gasp as she covered her mouth. (And weapons. What are they going to do? I have to hurry and catch up, but staying far enough behind so that I will not be seen.

Judas went before them, and drew near to Jesus to kiss him. This was his signal to the others that this was Jesus.)

But Jesus said to him, "Judas, are you betraying the Son of man with a kiss?"

When the other disciples saw what would follow, they said to him, "Lord, should we go after them with the sword?"

Peter drew his sword and cut off the ear of one of the men.

Jesus said calmly to Peter, "Put the sword back in the sheathe. I have to do what my Father has sent me to do."

Then she heard Jesus say, "Who are you looking for?"

They answered, "Jesus of Nazareth."

Jesus said, "I am he."

Then he asked again, "Who are you looking for?"

And they said, "Jesus of Nazareth."

Jesus answered, "I have told you that I am he. If I am the one you want, let the rest of these go their way."

(What are they going to do to Jesus?), Mary Magdalen thought to herself.

He touched the servant's ear and healed him.

Mary Magdalen was puzzled, (What are they going to do to my Master now?)

Then the group took Jesus and bound him.

(They are taking him away. I must follow. I cannot let anything bad happen to my Lord.)

Mary Magdalen followed a safe distance behind the band of adversaries.

(Hmm. They are taking him to Annas. He is the Father-In-Law of Caiaphas, which is the High Priest)

Mary Magdalen remembered that one man should die for the people.

She could see that Simon Peter was following close behind Jesus. However, he did not go in with him. She did not go in either. She kept a close eye on Peter.

The girl that kept the door, said to Peter, "Are you also one of this man's disciples?"

And he said to her, "I am not."

Mary Magdalen said to herself, (Of course he is one of Jesus's disciples. He has been with him since before me.)

The servants and officers stood outside. They had made a fire of coals, because it was cold, and they warmed themselves. And Peter stood with them and warmed himself.

Mary Magdalen pulled her shawl tight around her shoulders. Yes, it was getting cold. (How could Peter deny Jesus? He was his number one Apostle.)

One of the men who stood and warmed himself with the servant asked, "Are you one of his disciples?"

He denied it and said, "I am not."

Again Mary Magdalen could not understand how Peter could deny the Christ.

Another of the servants of the high priest, being related to the one whose ear was cut off said, "Did I see you in the garden with him?"

Peter again denied the fact that he was with Jesus in the garden, and immediately the cock crew,

(Peter had denied knowing and being with Jesus three times. And he ran off sobbing. I do not understand any of this. I would never deny my Lord and Savior.)

* * * * *

The girl, who had been in the room where Jesus was taken, came out and Mary Magdalen asked, "Do you know where Jesus has been taken?"

She answered, "I think I heard them say they were taking him to Caiaphas to be interrogated."

Mary Magdalen went as fast as she could to the hall of judgement.

She stood outside for quite a while, listening to the crowd saying that Jesus should be crucified. She had heard of crucifixions, but she had never witnessed one. She knew they could not crucify the Lord. God would protect him.

* * * * *

Jesus was led from Caiaphas to the hall of judgement. And it was early.

And Jesus stood before the governor, Pontius Pilate. And the governor asked him, saying, "Are you the King of the Jews?" And Jesus said to him, "You say so."

When he sat down on the judgement seat, his wife went to him saying, "Have nothing to do with that just man. For I have suffered many things this day in a dream because of him."

But the chief priests and elders persuaded the multitude that they should release Barabbas and destroy Jesus.

Pilate said to them, "What shall I do with Jesus which is called Christ?"

They all said to him, "Let him be crucified."

Pilate then went out to them and asked, "What is he accused of?"

And the Jews said, "If he were not a malefactor, we would not have delivered him up at this time."

Then Pilate said, "Take him, and judge him according to your law."

The Jews said to him, "It is not lawful for us to put any man to death."

Then Pilate called Jesus to him and asked, "Are you the King of the Jews?"

Jesus answered him, "Do you say this by yourself, or did others tell you about me?"

Pilate asked, "Am I a Jew? Your own nation and the chief priests have delivered you to me. What have you done?"

Jesus answered, "My kingdom is not of this world. If my kingdom were of this world, then would my servant's fight, that I should not be taken to the Jews, but now is my kingdom not from here."

Pilate said to him, "Are you a king then?"

Jesus answered, "You say I am a king. This was why I was born, and this is why I came into the world. That I should bear witness of the truth. Every one that is of the truth hears my voice."

Everyone who was in the Hall of Judgement and in front of it heard every word that was spoken by Pilate and Jesus. They all listened intently to hear what each one had to say.

Pilate continued, "What is the truth?" And when he had said this, he walked in front of the Jews, and said to them, "I do not find any fault in him at all. But you have a custom, that I should release one at the Passover. Would you want me to release to you the King of the Jews?"

Then they all cried again saying, "Not this man, but Barabbas."

Now Barabbas was a robber.

Most of the people in the crowd wanted Barabbas freed and Jesus hung.

Mary Magdalen was in the crowd. She knew Jesus was innocent of any crime. She could not say anything for fear of being sent out and stoned. So she said nothing, but stood and sobbed. No one paid any attention to her because they were too busy condemning Jesus.

* * * * *

Then Pilate took Jesus inside of the building and scourged him. And the soldiers made a crown of thorns and placed it on his head. And they put a purple robe on him.

And they said, "Hail, King of the Jews." And they slapped him with their hands.

Pilate went again before the people and said, "Behold, I bring him out to you, that you may know I find no fault in him."

When Pilate saw that he could prevail nothing, he took water, and washed his hands before the multitude, saying, "I am innocent of the blood of this just person. See to it."

Then Jesus came in front of the crowd wearing the crown of thorns, and the purple robe. And Pilate said, "Behold the man!"

Then answered all the people, and said, "His blood be on us, and on our children."

Then he released Barabbas to them. He delivered Jesus to be crucified.

And Pilate gave sentence that it should be as they desired.

* * * * *

And as they led him away, they laid hold upon one Simon, a Cyrenian, coming out of the country, and on him they laid the cross, that he might bear it when Jesus was too weak.

And there followed with him a lot of people. Mary Magdalen and many other women wailed all the way to Golgotha.

A great company of people followed him.

But Jesus turning to them said, "Daughters of Jerusalem, weep not for me, but weep for yourselves, and for your children."

There was a man named Joseph, a counsellor, and he was a just and good man.

Joseph of Arimathaea, went to Pilate, and begged for the body of Jesus.

And when they came to the place, which is called Calvary, there they crucified him, and the malefactors, one on the right hand, and the other on the left.

Then Jesus said, "Father, forgive them, for they know not what they do." Meaning the Jews.

And the people stood watching. And the rulers also with them saying, "He saved others; let him save himself, if he be Christ, the chosen of God."

And the soldiers also mocked him, coming to him, and offering him vinegar to drink. And saying, "If you be the king of the Jews, save yourself."

And Pilate wrote over him in Greek, Latin, and Hebrew, THIS IS THE KING OF THE JEWS.

This title was read by many of the Jews, for the place where Jesus was crucified was close to the city.

Then the chief priests of the Jews said to Pilate, "Do not write, The King of the Jews."

Pilate answered, "What I have written, I have written.

* * * * *

And one of the malefactors looked at Jesus and said, "If you be Christ, save yourself and us."

But the other answered saying, "You should fear God because you are in the same condemnation. And we indeed justly; for we receive the due reward of our deeds; but this man has done nothing wrong."

And he said to Jesus, "Lord, remember me when you come into your kingdom."

And Jesus said to him, "Today you will be with me in paradise."

* * * * *

It was about the sixth hour, and there was a darkness which covered all of the earth until the ninth hour. The sun was darkened, and the veil of the temple was torn in the middle.

Now there stood by the cross of Jesus, Jesus's mother and his mother's sister, Mary the wife of Cleophas, and Mary Magdalen.

When Jesus saw his mother, and John standing by, he said to his mother, "Woman behold your son!"

Then he said to John, "Behold your mother."

From that hour, John took her to his home.

When Jesus had cried with a loud voice, he said, "Father into your hands I commend my spirit." And having said that he gave up the ghost.

And it started to rain.

Then they crucified him, and parted his garments, and upon his robe they cast lots.

Now when the centurion saw what was done, he glorified God, saying, "Certainly this was a righteous man."

Peter denies knowing Jesus three times is found in the New Testament John 18:17-18

Jesus repairs servant's Ear is found in the New Testament Luke 22:50-51

Jesus's trial is found in the New Testament John 19:1-14

The man who carried the cross is found in the New Testament Luke 23:26

Jesus said Forgive them for they know not what they do is found in the New Testament Luke 23:33

Solders mock and give him vinegar to drink is found in the New Testament Luke 23:36

Malefactors remarks is found in the New Testament Luke 23:39-43

The soldiers parted his garments is found in the New Testament Matthew 27:35

In the Gospel of Philip Mary Magdalen was considered a partner, an associate, and a companion.

Chapter Nine

BURIAL AND FURTHER MINISTRY

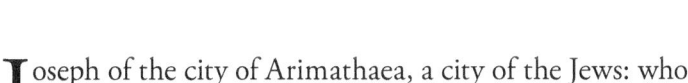

Joseph of the city of Arimathaea, a city of the Jews: who also himself waited for the kingdom of God. And he took the body down, and wrapped it in linen, and laid it in a sepulcher that was hewn stone, wherein never before was man laid.

And that day was the preparation, and the Sabbath drew on.

"I must see where they lay my Lord," Mary Magdalen said as she sobbed. "Sisters, please come with me. I must bring ointments so he can have a proper burial."

And the women also, beside Mary Magdalen, which came with him from Galilee, followed after, and beheld the sepulcher, and how his body was laid.

"I do not know if I can do this", Mary stated. "He is my son. I gave birth to him. I have followed him through much of his ministry. How can I prepare his body for his final burial?"

"You can do it. You must be strong. It is our duty to see that his burial is the best that we can do, He deserves only the best," was Mary Magdalen's rebuttal.

"He was a magnificent man. He did miracles nobody else could have done. I have never heard of anyone else that could restore life to those who were dead, cleanse lepers, bring sight to the blind, make the lame to walk, cast out demons and so many other things, and all in three short years."

"You are right, Mary Magdalen, I have been thinking only of my own selfishness. Preparing him for his burial is the last act I can do for him."

* * * * *

And they returned, and prepared spices and ointments; and rested the Sabbath day according to the commandment.

Among the women was, Mary Magdalen, and Mary the mother of James and Joses, Jesus's mother Mary and the mother of Zebedee's children.

* * * * *

Now the next day that followed the day of the preparation, the chief priests and Pharisees came together to see Pilate, saying, "Sir, we remember that that deceiver said, while he was yet alive, 'After three days I will rise again.'

"Command therefore that the sepulcher be made sure until the third day, lest his disciples come by night, and steal him away, and shall be worse than the first."

Pilate said to them, "You have a watch. Go your way, and make it as sure as you can."

So they went, and made the sepulcher sure, sealing the stone in front of the entrance to the sepulcher and put two soldiers to watch.

Roman governors almost never allowed for executed criminals to be given any kind of burial and kindly asked by a member of the Jewish council to provide a decent burial for a crucified victim.

* * * * *

At the end of the Sabbath, as it began to be dawn toward the first day of the week, they came to the sepulcher at the rising of the sun. Then came Mary Magdalen and another Mary to see the sepulcher.

"Who will roll the stone from the tomb?" Mary Magdalen asked.

And there was a great earthquake. For the angel of the Lord descended from heaven, and came and rolled back the stone from the door, and sat on it.

His countenance was like lightening, and his raiment was white as snow. The other Mary ran away because she was afraid.

And for fear of him the soldiers, who were the watchers, did shake, and left their swords and ran away and never looked back.

And when Mary Magdalen saw that the stone was rolled away she entered.

And entering the sepulcher, she saw an angel. She was frightened.

And the angel said to the woman, "Fear not. For I know that you seek Jesus, which was crucified. He is not here. For he has risen, as he said. Come, see the place where the Lord did lay."

And she went out quickly, for she trembled and was amazed. And she fled quickly. She did not say anything to any man because she was afraid.

* * * * *

When Jesus was risen early the first day of the week, he appeared first to Mary Magdalen.

Now alone in the garden outside the tomb, Jesus approached her. At first she mistook him for the gardener, but, after she heard him say her name, she recognized him and cried out "Rabboni!" (which is Aramaic for "teacher")

He then said, "Do not touch me, for I have not yet ascended to my Farther".

And she went and told the disciples that she had been with him, as they mourned and wept.

And when they had heard he was alive and that she had seen him, they did not believe her.

* * * * *

As they went to see, Jesus met them, and saying, "All hail." And they came and held him by the feet, and worshipped him.

Then Jesus said to them, "Be not afraid. Go tell my brethren that they go to Galilee, and there will they see me."

Then the eleven disciples went to Galilee and into a mountain where Jesus had sent them.

And when they saw him, they worshipped him. But some doubted.

And Jesus came and spoke to them, saying, "All power is given to me in heaven and in earth."

Mary Magdalen followed the disciples to Galilee and listened intently to the instructions he gave.

* * * * *

Teaching them to observe all things I have commanded you. I am with you always, even to the end of the world.

* * * * *

Now when the soldiers which had the watch over the sepulcher, came into the city, and showed to the chief priests all the things that had happened.

Mary Magdalen tells the other disciples, who are all in fright for their own lives: "Do not weep or grieve or be in doubt, for his grace will be with you all and will protect you. Rather, let us praise his greatness, for he has prepared us and made us truly human."

Peter approaches Mary and asks her, "Sister we know that the Savior loved you more than the rest of the women. Tell us the words of the Savior which you remember which you know, but we do not, nor have we heard them".

Mary answered and said, "What is hidden from you I will proclaim to you". And she began to speak to them these words, "I", She said, "I saw you today in a vision.

Mary then proceeds revealing that she is the only one who has understood Jesus's true teachings. Andrew, the Apostle challenged Mary insisting, "Say what you think about what she said, but I do not believe the Savior said this. These teachings are strange ideas."

Peter responds saying, "Did he really speak with a woman in private, without our knowledge? Should we all listen to her? Did he prefer her to us?"

Andrew and Peter's responses are intended to demonstrate that they do not understand Jesus's teachings and that it is really only Mary who truly understands.

Matthew, the Apostle, comes to Mary's defense, giving a sharp rebuke to Peter. "Peter, you are always angry. Now I see you arguing against this woman like an adversary. If the Savior made her worthy, who are you to reject her? Surely the Savior knows her well. That is why he loved her more than us."

* * * * *

When they were all together, and the elders had taken counsel, they gave a large amount of money to the soldiers, saying, "Say that his disciples came by night, and stole him away while we slept. And if it comes to the governor's ears, we will persuade him, and you will not be blamed."

* * * * *

When the eleven disciples went away to Galilee, upon a mountain where Jesus had sent them. And when they saw him they worshipped him. But Thomas doubted.

And Jesus came and spoke to them, saying, "All power is given to me in heaven and in earth."

Mary Magdalen listened as he gave instructions, "Go into all the world, and preach the gospel to every creature.

"He that believes and is baptized will be saved. But he that does not believe will be damned."

"And these signs will follow them that believe, in my name they will cast out devils and they will be able to speak with new tongues. They will take up serpents, and if they drink any deadly thing, it will not hurt them. They will lay hands on the sick, and they will recover."

* * * * *

So then after the Lord had spoken to them, he was received up into heaven, and sat on the right hand of God.

Jesus buried in the tomb of Joseph of Arimathaea is found in the New Testament Luke 23:50-56

Women ministering to Jesus is found in the New Testament Matthew 27:55-56

Jesus not in sepulcher is found in the New Testament Mark 16:2-11

Jesus appeared to the eleven is found in the New Testament Mark 16:14

Instructions to the disciples is found in the New Testament Mark 16:15-18

Going to Galilee is found in the New Testament Matthew 28:16-18

Jesus sits on the right hand of God is found in the New Testament Mark 16:19